Contents

HUMAN MECHANISMS OF FAILURE TO SUCCESS

Understanding the Forces Behind Every Outcome

K. KRISHNANANDA

ISBN

Paperback 979-8-89724-504-8
Hardcase 979-8-89744-872-2

Preface

There might be hardly anyone in the world that has not experienced the joy of success or the sorrow of failure, whether that success or failure is big or small. Success and failure are concepts that define much of our lives. We measure success in accomplishments, wealth, relationships, and recognition, and define failure as a lack of achievement or falling short of our expectations. However, as I delved deeper into these two forces, I began to realize that success and failure are not simply external events; they are the results of complex, internal mechanisms at work within us.

Every human being has special and extraordinary qualities that we need to develop and leverage to improve our chances of success.

I wrote this book to explore and share these mechanisms, the invisible systems that govern the way we experience success and failure. For too long, our focus has been on surface-level actions such as strategies, tactics, and behaviors, but what if the real cause of success or failure lies deeper beneath the surface of our conscious actions; in the beliefs, thoughts, and energies that guide us? This is what I sought to understand and ultimately share with you.

First and for most, I would like to praise and bow down to the lotus feet of Sri Sri Sri Satya Ananta Madhav Maha Prabhu, who has granted countless blessing so that I have been able to accomplish the book.

Special thanks to my family, sister Sandhya Prabhu, and express my deep sense of gratitude to friends Tilak Raj Jaisingh, Hardik Sodha, Kanan Joshi, Simran Thakur for their support and encouragement resulted in completion of this book.

Introduction

This book, *HUMAN MECHANISMS OF FAILURE TO SUCCESS*, presents a new perspective that goes beyond conventional thinking. Success is not merely a matter of hard work and luck; it is the product of inner alignment, the harmony between our thoughts, emotions, beliefs, and the actions we take. Similarly, failure is not an unavoidable outcome; it is often the result of misalignment within our internal world- the unseen barriers, doubts, and emotional blocks that prevent us from reaching our full potential.

I have shared the facts about how we create obstacles for ourselves and how we can be aware of our mistakes, which attract failure in life. Through this book, one will understand the barriers to being a natural, free, spontaneous, creative, wise, and intelligent person. It is a unique expression of universal flow hindered by our knowing and unknowing thoughts, patterns, and actions.

It is important to understand the reason why and how we become the source of our complete destruction, failure, or success. The book also emphasizes opportunities and ways to use failure and move toward success.

This book will focus on the mechanism for living a successful, beautiful, and fulfilling life with freedom. This mechanism is the secret of manifestation in the creation of human beings. It helps one understand where they may be going wrong or where they lack in achieving true well-being and success. Whether one is pursuing spirituality, working to achieve business success, or building meaningful relationships, understanding this mechanism can reveal where one may be stuck.

The right guidance at the right time is required for all beings; this book is just a small step and effort to bring that light into people's lives and show them the path of complete transformation and creation.

In the end, we also mentioned the exceptional recreational retreats offered by the author for personalized coaching and learning advanced techniques to achieve success and fulfill your desire.

Testimonials

The Retreat conducted by Shri Krishnanandaji played a vital role in my spiritual journey, and later on as I came to realise, in my personal and professional life as well. I attended Krishnanandji's retreat, a decade after starting my spiritual journey. At first, I felt that perhaps there is not much for me to learn here, after all I had already attended many other meditation programs including some which required one to maintain many day's silence. This short retreat helped me get over some thing the other programs did not - Fear of Failure, which was impeding my personal and professional growth. A combination of group activities, meditation sessions and personal time spent with Krishnanandji at the Retreat brought clarity into how to achieve my goal and fulfil my life's purpose.

Aniruddh Rao, marine engineer
Mumbai.

Having gone through various spiritual disciplines and after hearing to various gurus, I gained a lot of intellectual understanding, but I couldn't find the peace and stoppage of mind. Doing satsanga weekly, doing lots of service and meditating daily with strict diet , I felt something was missing. I understood that going beyond actions which are time and place bound cannot happen by action itself. Luckily I met Krishnanandaji by divine grace and he asked me to join his retreat. When I started the journey to ashram near Narmada river bank, I found the nature supporting me like never before.

In the retreat program, Krishnananda ji made all the participants to experience the emptiness by WHO AM I method, because of which for the first time in my life I could feel total dissolution of the mind without any kind of self effort just by divine grace. It seemed as the divine was making Krishnanandji an instrument and delivering knowledge through him. Because of Krishnananda ji's wisdom and guidance I could get myself rid of false ideologies and experienced what reality is. Observing his life, I learnt how to live with the Truth and tackle various kinds of problems in my life. Whenever there is any problems in my life, Krishnanandji is always available to give his valuable advice. His timely advice and intervention had a very positive effect on my goal and family.

Rishi Ramesh Soni
B.E. Instrumentation engineering,
CNC expert, Gold jewellery manufacturing.

Raised in a spiritually inclined family, I was exposed to various spiritual practices from a young age. Spanning multiple years, I happen to connect with Krishnanandji, who was hosting a retreat. I was drawn to attend the retreat, and this encounter proved to be a pivotal moment in my spiritual journey and life. Attending the retreat was a watershed moment, imbuing me with crystalline clarity on my goals and vision. The retreat empowered me to be stronger, happier, and more resilient.

Krishnanand ji presence in my life has been a divine blessing. He instinctively senses when I am struggling and offers guidance without needing explanation. His spiritual and practical guidance in my life has helped me thrive amidst adversity.

Aashka Hardik Sodha
Lead Safety Consultant (Food Safety & Health and Safety)

Krishnanandaji association has been with ages now and every form I have transcended it feels like, he has also been guiding lighting one way or other wayin this life time too, his profound teachings had deep impact in spirituality and in my daily life. His retreats have made me realise the being of being , connecting the wandering mind and clarity in my vision to being with such simple and yet very powerful guidance his wisdom has also helped me explore more in this thirst full journey.

Sunil Venkatesh B.E , M.Tech , LL.B
Legal Consultant.
Certified Yoga Teacher
Ministry of Ayush , Govt Of INDIA.

Human Mechanisms

Spirituality and materialism are often seen as two separate aspects, and when we focus simply on one of them, it can lead to imbalance. Materialism is necessary for the body's survival and well-being. However, the experience of being and the natural state is not possible without the body. For a responsible person, it is crucial to live successfully and to be in a state of well-being. While the expression of life and the results of living may differ from person to person, the underlying mechanism behind it remains the same. The universal function through the body is constant, but the outcomes and expressions are unique to everyone. We have the freedom to choose how we want to express ourselves and live.

Successful individuals are not always truly appreciated by their loved ones because they lack a natural essence. Often, they create suffering for themselves due to their limitations. Nature does not intend for anyone to suffer, as there is no suffering in Brahma Tattva (the Ultimate Truth). One can either keep things as they are or change them using the power of freewill by understanding this mechanism. This mechanism is for those who seek success, not for those who are content with their current situation. It is the system that governs both our inner and outer worlds. It is the secret to create and live our life's purpose.

Many of us are in the process of spirituality, building careers, or cultivating meaningful relationships, but we often feel stuck. We don't know why we're not progressing or achieving the desired success. The mechanism of life provides a way to understand what's holding us back. It helps us identify where we are out of alignment with our true self and shows us the path to real success.

Panch Kosha – Five Shells of Human Existence

Kosha is a Sanskrit term that means "sheath" or "layer" and is used in yogic philosophy to describe the different layers or aspects of human existence. **There are five main koshas in human mechanisms. Annamaya kosha** (Physical Body), **Pranamayakosha** (Energy Body), **Monamayakosha (Mental Body),Vijnanamaya Kosha** (Wisdom Body), **Anandamaya Kosha** (Bliss Body). These layers are thought to enclose the true self, or **Atman(soul),** much like an onion has multiple layers. Like Panchkosha we also has Panchpranas such as prana, apana, vyana, udhana, samana; these pachaprana is the source to function the body.

The koshas highlight the interdependence of physical health, mental clarity, and spiritual contentment. By integrating all koshas, desires can manifest in a way that not only fulfills personal goals, but also aligns with universal harmony and deeper satisfaction.

For example:

Stress in the **Manomaya Kosha** (mental body) can manifest as physical ailments in the **Annamaya Kosha**.

A healthy, balanced **Pranamaya Kosha** (energy body) can boost mental and emotional well-being.

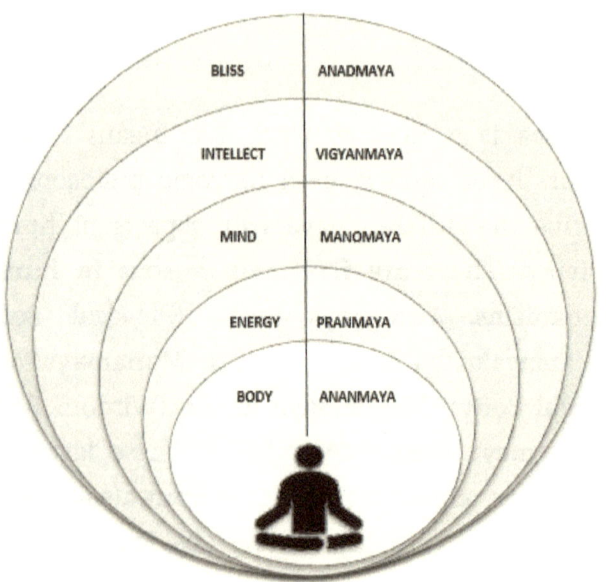

TYPE OF KOSHA:

1. **Annamaya Kosha (Physical Body)**

   - It is the outermost layer and the easiest to perceive and nurture.

   - Represents the gross physical body, sustained by food (Anna means food).

- This is the tangible aspect of our existence, including muscles, bones, and organs.

2. **Pranamaya Kosha (Energy or Prana Body)**

   - Represents the vital life force or energy (Prana) that animates the physical body.

   - Includes the breath and the subtle energies that flow through nadis (energy channels) and chakras and fuels every action in the physical body.

3. **Manomaya Kosha (Mental Body)**

   - This Kosha takes a lead role in human mechanism.

   - It represents the mind or mental layer, emotions, thoughts, feelings, and sensory experiences or desires reside. This is where the seeds of manifestation are planted. Impressions are captured and give rise to desires.

4. **Vijnanamaya Kosha (Wisdom Body)**

   - The layer of judgment, higher wisdom, and guiding intentions, and aligning them with universal truths. (Vijnana means knowledge).

   - It involves intuition, self-reflection, and the ability to distinguish truth from illusion.

5. **Anandamaya Kosha (Bliss Body)**

- The innermost layer, the sheath of pure joy and connection with the infinite. A state of oneness with creation.

- It is characteristic of bliss, tranquility, containment, love, joy and cheerfulness.

FUNCTIONS OF KOSHA:

The physical gross body (Annamay) can be seen and touched, but behind the physical body other subtle layers of kosha (Pranamay, Monamaya, Vigyanmay, Annadmay) cannot be seen or touched, but it can be experienced by every individual. Because of these subtle layers one can think, move, and act accordingly.

These layers guide our actions, define our reality, and direct the flow of energy in our lives. If the foundational structure of these layers is complex, then that complexity governs how they function and impact. And this can be expressed through the Panchakosha (five Sheaths) the five interconnected layers such as physical, energetic, mental, intellectual and spiritual.

Each kosha (layers) influences the others, determining how we experience the world and how effectively we manifest our desires.

When these koshas are in harmony, manifestation flows effortlessly. When out of balance, they create blocks that block the process. The body (Annamaya Kosha) acts as the foundation, energy (Pranamaya Kosha) fuels the process, thoughts (Manomaya Kosha) shape desires, wisdom (Vigyanamaya Kosha) guides intention, and bliss (Anandamaya Kosha) connects us to the infinite source of possibilities.

EXAMPLE:

The dead person has all the parts of body and organs, but it cannot act or move on its own because the soul along with the other four layers (kosha) has departed. And hence we identify it as dead.

A person in coma has its **Annamaya Kosha** (body) and **Pranamaya Kosha** (energy) functioning, but at a minimal level, often sustained by medical support. However, the **Manomaya Kosha** (mind), **Vijnanamaya Kosha** (intellect), and **Anandamaya Kosha** (bliss) are inactive and not functioning. As a result, desires from the mind, guidance from the intellect, and enjoyment from bliss cannot be expressed through the body because the person is in an unconscious state.

Layers of kosha: Positive, Negative, and Lowest:

Human life functions across several dimensions (Layers of Consciousness, Panchakosha), influenced by our state of being whether it's positive, negative, or the lowest. These dimensions are interconnected and reveal how our emotions, thoughts, and energy affect our mental and physical health, as well as the direction in which our life is taking shape.

Layers of existence	Positive	Negative	Lowest
Bliss (Anand)	Blissful state	Sadness	Dullness
Intellect (Vigyan)	Stable	Confused	Foolish
Mind (Maan)	Detached	Attached	Depressed
Energy (Prana)	Energetic	Lowest energy	Inertia (Laziness)
Physical Body (Food)	Healthy	Illness	Deceased

Positive State:

In a positive state, we feel inspired, energetic, and open to opportunities. Even when faced with challenges, the mind remains clear, and the spirit resilient. Sustained positivity not only leads to personal success but also has a ripple effect, inspiring and uplifting others around you. By maintaining a positive mindset, individuals can create an environment where success multiplies and benefits a larger community.

Negative State:

In a negative state, things slow down. When one remains negative over time, their attitude can impact those around them, causing others to feel upset or challenged. When negativity continues, they may struggle because of it and feel anxious or stuck, but there is still the possibility of recovery.

Lowest State of Negativity:

However, when negativity reaches its lowest point, it becomes more than just a feeling, it transforms into a state of mental illness. In this state, a person may experience emotional numbness, extreme fatigue, and a deep sense of hopelessness, and may commit suicide. The lowest state can erode both physical and mental health, leading to dangerous consequences if left unchecked.

The Impact of Emotional Trauma on Manomaya Kosha:

Manomaya Kosha, the layer governing thoughts, emotions, and desires, is especially vulnerable to emotional disturbances. When trauma or chronic stress takes hold, this sheath reacts by:

- Allowing negative thoughts to dominate, reinforcing limiting beliefs.

- Harboring unresolved emotions such as fear, anger, or sadness can cloud clarity and create inner conflict.

- Attaching to past experiences, leading to cycles of anxiety and reactive behaviors, which prevents focus on present intentions.

- One avoid situations, people, or places. Mood swings, irritability, or feelings of intense sadness, anxiety, or anger are common symptoms. Also, one with emotional trauma may withdraw from social interactions, isolate themselves from family or friends, and lose interest in activities they once enjoyed.

For instance, someone who has experienced failure in an important endeavor might internalize the belief, "I am incapable of success." When left unaddressed, this belief becomes a lens through which all future experiences are filtered, perpetuating self-doubt and undermining efforts to manifest positive outcomes.

How Trauma Ripples Through the Koshas:

1. Monamaya Kosha (Mind)

   Although Manomaya Kosha is the initial layer affected by emotional trauma, its influence extends across the other koshas, manifesting in other layers as mentioned below.

2. Annamaya Kosha (Physical Body):

   The body often reflects the strain of unresolved repeated emotions. Stress can manifest as tension, chronic fatigue, or physical illness, creating disconnect between mind and body.

3. Pranamaya Kosha (Vital Energy):

   Trauma disrupts the flow of prana (life force), resulting in lethargy, and lack of motivation, rejection to move and a sensation of being "stuck." This stagnation impairs the creative processes essential for manifestation.

4. Vijnanamaya Kosha (Wisdom Body):

   Emotional distress clouds the intellect, diminishing our ability to access discernment and higher wisdom. This can lead to poor decision-making, confusion, wrong justice and misalignment with our true purpose.

5. Anandamaya Kosha (Bliss Body):

   Prolonged stress creates a sense of separation from joy and fulfillment. This disconnection from our innermost bliss inhibits our ability to align with the infinite source of creation, leaving us feeling isolated, shrinking and unfulfilled.

The Belief System

"Whether you think you can or you think you can't, you're right."

– *Henry Ford*

What one belief, one becomes.

A **confirming conclusion** can be drawn that **past events, whether positive or negative, impact all layers of the kosha system** and are stored in memory as part of our **belief system**. This stored memory becomes the blueprint of how we perceive ourselves, others, and the world.

Whether good or bad, our experiences, emotions, and actions affect the entire body through sensations. The impact on all layers of the body forms a memory, which solidifies into the belief system.

Good past events bring positive beliefs, which leads to confidence. Bad past events bring negative beliefs, which leads to fear and insecurity.

For example: What one believes about their roles in life—whether as a mother, father, son, daughter, sister, brother, uncle, or aunt—does not require any reminding from anyone. They blindly believe in and perform their duties towards their role.

Belief works in every human life, whether it is positive or negative. Every action is based on one's belief, for instance, someone daring to stand and give a speech in public or choosing to decline due to shyness.

Example:

A child has a frightening encounter with an aggressive street dog. The memory of the dog barking, growling, or even biting is just a record of what happened. But the interpretation, the belief that "dogs are dangerous" emerges from how the child processes that experience. This interpretation stays with the child, coloring their perception of dogs.

The next time this child sees a dog that belief will resurface. If the dog barks or growls, the belief is reinforced: "Yes, dogs are indeed dangerous." With each repeated experience that aligns with this interpretation, the belief solidifies further.

On the other hand, if a person has pleasant experience with the dog that memory will generate a repetitive experience of dogs are friendly being and the belief solidifies.

Belief works in every aspect of life whether it is positive or negative. Every action is based or is an outcome of one's beliefs, for example, someone chooses to take the challenge or hide out due to fear of failing.

Any masters or athletics coach has techniques to remove fear from their students easily and they don't give much importance to realize how much fear student have; however, the coach will slowly raise students' trust, confidence and encourage tosuch level to focus on their goals.

Belief is the basic part of our intellectual behavior which helps us to achieve our goals with the proper decisions.

Similarly, if one holds beliefs rooted in fear about finances, relationships, health, or business, they are likely to experience financial crises, toxic relationships, health issues, and struggles in business.

Knowingly or unknowingly, whatever happens in one's life is a reflection of their inner beliefs. Achievers attain success because they strongly believe in their intentions and goals. The belief system is a powerful tool in human existence, that is possessing the ability to attract from nature whatever is needed to achieve those goals. Whatever one believes, they naturally carry the associated emotions within themselves—be it fear, doubt, or confidence—and they act in alignment with those emotions.

For example, the frequencies of all radio channels are present in the space, but only the one that is tuned in is played on the radio.

Similarly, in all the aspects of life like business, health, relationships, what one is carrying as a strong belief in his memory that same situation will be attracted through nature.

Just as in radio frequency example, whatever one carries as a strong belief within, one will attract the same thoughts and situations frequently in life.

Nature also brings similar situations to help us overcome the deeply rooted, limited impressions within us. It seeks to teach us a lesson—that negative impressions can be transformed.

All successful achievers first believed that they could achieve their goal and then dreamed about it every movement or practiced every day because they believed they could achieve it one day. If we have a strong belief system, then we can do the most difficult tasks.

Example: In earlier times, there used to be great enlightened gurus (spiritual masters) who had achieved immense spiritual powers **(siddhis)**, and they used these powers for the welfare of humanity. Seeing the power of these gurus, many people would come to them to become their disciples and learn from them. To teach such disciples, the gurus would impart special mantras, known as **Beej Mantras** (seed mantras).

However, gurus would not give these mantras to everyone; they were only bestowed upon those who were deemed eligible. This is because chanting these mantras involved specific and complex practices, which were not easy to follow. The gurus would carefully identify deserving disciples and grant them these mantras.

The *Beej Mantra* acts as a seed for attaining spiritual powers and serves as the foundation for achieving great siddhis in the future.

When a guru selects a deserving disciple and bestows the mantra upon them, the disciple feels honored and believes that the guru has chosen them from among many others. With this strong sense of **trust**, the disciple diligently follows the practices taught by the guru and works on the **Beej Mantra**.

Because of their unwavering faith in the guru, the disciple eventually attains **siddhis** (spiritual powers) like those of the guru. In this field, it is the disciple's unshakable faith in the guru that elevates them to the highest levels of spiritual attainment. This is how belief system makes one achieve their goal or vision.

A Real story of Anurima Sinha:

Anurima is an Indian mountaineer and sportswoman. On April 11, 2011, she was traveling on the Padmavati Express from Lucknow to Delhi to attend an exam. That night, while she was on the train, a group of robbers tried to steal her gold chain. When she restricted, they pushed her out of the moving train. She fell onto the tracks, and another train coming from the opposite direction ran over her leg below the knee.

She cried for help all night, but no one came to her rescue. Rats gnawed at her injured leg throughout the night. The next morning, she was taken to the hospital, but the doctors at AIIMS said it would take at least 3 to 4 years for her to recover fully.

However, Anurima took it as a challenge and proved that **"A person is handicapped by their body, not by their mind."**

After two years, she applied for mountaineering training under Madam Bachendri Pal. Hearing her story; Madam Pal was moved to tears and told her, "You are already a winner in your mind; now it's time to show the world."

After eight months of rigorous training, on May 21, 2013, Anurima became the first Indian female amputee to scale Mount Everest. She successfully reached the summit and hoisted the Indian flag, inspiring millions with her determination and courage. **Arunima is the first India's female amputee to scale Mount Everest.**

Karma and Selection:

Nature knows numerous paths for us and presents us with the free will to choose from them. The course of a person's journey unfolds based on the selections they make. This concept can be understood as a tree or lineage; the path chosen influences the entire trajectory of one's life and the generations that follow.

We misunderstand the concept of Karma and throw the entire blame on destiny. But our destiny is largely shaped by the choices we make. The suffering and lessons associated with Karma are experienced regardless of the path taken. Therefore, selecting a positive path may help us mitigate the hardships reflected on us through our karma.

However, the foundation of our choices is crucial. If our decisions arise from negative emotions such as fear, anger, or revenge, these feelings will manifest along the chosen path.

Therefore, before making choices, it is essential to understand this mechanism and address any negative influences at our roots. While we often hear people recommend maintaining a positive attitude, managing anger, and eliminating negative emotions, the question remains—how can we achieve this?

The answer lies in a powerful observation technique called Murdhini Prana, mentioned in the last chapter.

Uprooting the negative belief and redesigning the belief system:

A tree infected by the pests must be treated at the roots, not through the branches. Similarly, in life, we often focus on the branches, but the real need is to perfect the roots.

When you search within yourself, the searcher remains. However, when you realize, nothing is left to search for, you begin to understand arrogance (Ahankar). It is like a thief searching for another thief—such contradictions highlight the untouched state of being. All work (karma) performed from this untouched space arises from beingness, which requires perfection at the roots.

For example, if you harbor fear, it will affect your cells, and fear will manifest further, becoming absorbed into every cell. Carrying such fear perpetuates its manifestation, creating a cycle.

The key is to completely dissolve what can be dissolved at the root level or transform what cannot.

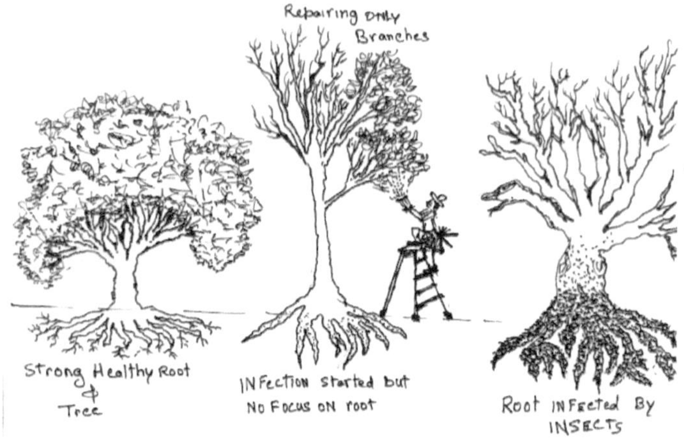

1.   *Strong Healthy rooted Tree:- Success*

2.   *Infection strated on root Tree:- People doesn't focus on correcting oneself but want's to corrects others and out siders.*

3.   *Already Infected Tree:- One will destroyed himself because of not paying attaintion to his negativity.*

Important Role of
Mind And Intellect

Do not listen to your mind blindly. First, ask yourself "Are you greater than your mind, or is your mind greater than you"?

Is your mind controlling you, or are you in control of your mind?

Do you belong to the mind, or is the mind merely one function of your existence?

Do you follow the mind, or are you aware of it?

The mind is different from the brain, the brain is a part of the physical body whereas the mind is abstract, and it is everywhere, we are in mind and mind is in us. Mind gives command to brain. The mind also collects impressions through five senses and stores it in the memory one of the layers of our existence.

The **mind** often seeks the easy path, comfort, laziness, postponement, compromise, and acceptance of failure. However, when we become aware of our mind, the power of a negative mindset diminishes.

This awareness allows our **intellect** to make decisive choices and move towards our goals. As a result, many new paths will open before us.

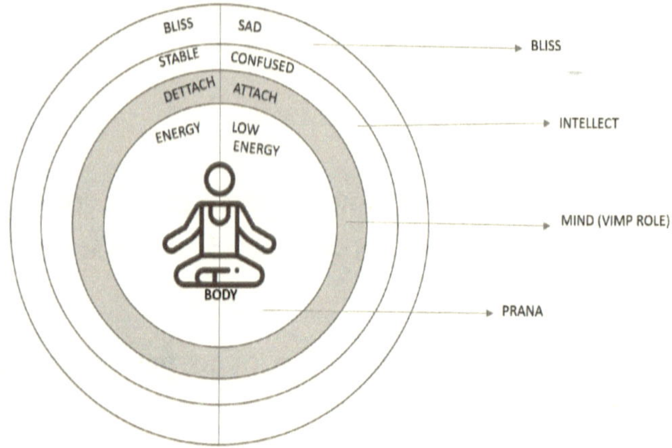

The mind is neither inside nor outside the body but surrounds it. It is connected to the brain and functions to give commands, which are accepted or rejected (either positively or negatively) by the other four layers (koshas) of body. Mind is a mediator between Physical body, Energy body and Intellect- Bliss. Mind will allow and it will play main role on one to have harmony between Physical body, Energy Body and Intellect-Bliss body.

Thoughts arise and are then filtered by the intellect. For instance, in the morning, you may have the thought to wake up, but your intellect might say, "Let's sleep a little longer." In that case, the mind enjoys the extra sleep. If the intellect continually dismisses the idea of waking up, no action will take place. Conversely, if the intellect decides to wake up and overrides the desire to stay in blissful sleep, it energizes you, leading to the action of getting out of bed.

The first thing required is harmony between mind and intellect; when both are in harmony then everything else and other layers are in harmony. Observe your continuity of thoughts to analyze whether you are stable or doubtful. Prana (energy), body, worldly life and way of living are just results. When the mind is in lack "I am not worthy of this or that, then it gets weaker and weaker. If instability crosses a certain level of weakness it will lead to depression and the next level might be suicide.

For inner world one can does not have any goal but in spirituality purpose of life is to know oneself. Achieving oneself is not a goal but to attain spirituality and material goal, this mechanism works. The body knows only to express whatever it may be action towards goal or relationship, family, business, etc.

When the body is in existence, there is action; interaction and dealing with the world for survival, and for this you need a clear direction (goal). How that goal (desire) will arise and bring a result, mechanism is a key to that function. Without proper direction one's fear and insecurity give rise to attachment, and hence forces one to live an obligatory life. If one is not clear about this mechanism and one's decision, then in this forceful living one will start blaming others for their past failures.

Body functions naturally on either side it is we who are giving power because of attached mind and judgmental intellect. One should not bother about small obstacles if one's goal is fixed with stability, belief and faith. Rather those small obstacles contribute towards success, however if the mind is doubtful every step will contribute towards failure. A stable intellect is not dependent on others for advice or decisions. One only runs behind the approvals if one is unstable. One even craves sympathy from others if one is not clear, perhaps is baffled with lots of questions and runs for the answers here and there.

Intuition will also work on the positive (stronger) side. Wishes would arise from a stronger side, and one prays intensely unknowingly; one has already handed it over, so there is no need to worry about stability or doubt; it is already given away to nature. Something has already been deleted there, so one is no longer working for it; there is no effort.

Realizing one's side in a situation is itself a process. Staying in a state of indecision leads to doubt. Stability comes when one makes a clear decision, saying, "I want to do this." It's important to just decide.

If someone ends up taking on the wrong project, a strong mindset can still allow them to learn from the experience. This learning will enable them to make better choices in the future, avoiding similar mistakes. Additionally, their intuition will begin to guide them in the right direction.

"If a person is in a natural state or free from inside, at the same time, he has made a resolution to do something without being bound to the body yet does not fulfill any of their duties even after making the resolution, nature will internally make them realize that they are not in the right place."

"The mind's job is to create desires and goals, while nature provides intuition to determine whether to act on them or not. If a desire arises that aligns with a role designated by the divine, the person will naturally feel inspired to pursue it. Like, if at a certain age someone listens to a successful singer and feels, 'I will become like this,' it may happen if becoming a singer is their destined role."

We often experience desires and intuitions about our destined roles from Nature, which can attract and interest us deeply. However, when we deny these feelings—often out of fear or due to past experiences—we may choose a different path. While this choice might initially bring some satisfaction, it often leads to a realization that we are not reaching our true potential. Also, when you are walking your destined path there may be struggle in the beginning, but later the flow will be effortless. When nature makes you do anything, first only toughness and challenges will come, so that all the negativity is released. During these tough times, it's important not to give up, and understand your future is bright in this direction.

For example: -"Pt. Bheemsen Joshi, a renowned Indian classical singer, left his home at the age of 11 to pursue his passion for singing. At that young age, he was inspired by Abdul Karim Khan's performance on the radio. In this situation, along with the strong willpower growing within the person, there was also God's will, which made achieving the goal easier.

If one is not attached, spontaneity comes at that moment to handle any situation. One on the negative side is living with fear. Understand, in naturalness also, one can be completely on the negative side because it is just a function of the body. In naturalness one is free and complete, there is no rush, but still, one wants to achieve something, then it is divine Sankalp. Nature wants contributions from this person to benefit humanity.

Role of Mind in Human Mechanisms:

The mind can hold beliefs, biases, and perspectives based on past conditioning. These beliefs guide behavior and influence how one interprets the world.

The mind also regulates and controls thoughts and actions through processes like self-discipline, focus, and willpower. It helps manage impulses and keeps behaviors in alignment with long-term goals.

The mind is the bridge between the conscious and subconscious mind. While the conscious mind controls deliberate actions, the subconscious mind influences automatic behaviors, habits, and responses.

The mind is also involved in spiritual practices and the pursuit of higher consciousness. It helps individuals to question, seek meaning, and connect with deeper aspects of existence.

The mind is essential in navigating all layers of the *koshas*, influencing physical health, energy flow, mental clarity, wisdom, and spiritual joy. The quality of the mind affects the state of each *kosha*, and through self-awareness and spiritual practices, the mind can be refined to move towards greater harmony, clarity, and deeper experiences of bliss.

If a person is confused, even if they are deeply involved in spirituality, progress may not happen because they are operating from the negative side. For example, consider some financially lower-class people who may not have a lavish life, but are stable in their approach. Their stability automatically places them on the positive side.

The outcome (expression) is a combination of worldly activities and the physical body. For instance, body and finances, or body and relationships, are part of a unified expression. What truly matters is the underlying force behind the expression. Nature simply reflects whatever one is carrying—positive energy results in positive outcomes, and negative energy leads to negative outcomes.

The mind plays a central role, while the body serves as its expression. The mind can focus on either the ultimate truth (Brahman or God) or worldly things. When the mind focuses on worldly things, it becomes attached to impermanent objects and experiences, mistaking them for the ultimate truth despite their transient nature.

On the other hand, when the mind shifts its attention to the observer (the self) and then to being (the natural, uninterrupted state), it realizes the power of the ultimate truth. This realization naturally brings stability, enabling the person to make clear decisions and maintain balance in all aspects of life.

Below table demonstrates the behavior of a stable and an unstable mind:

Confused and unstable Mind	Stable mind
Judgments, Comparison, Stressful Planning, worries, separation and sinful secrets	Clear thoughts,
Fearful Living	Fearless Living
Thinking about Past and Future	Transparency
Plans and Worries	Joy
Judgments	Love
Jealousy	Bliss
Hidings	Actions
Anger & screaming	no intrusive thoughts
Depression	Insightful Vision
Illness	
Accumulation & Holdings	
Waiting for Results	
Always Working	
Short Temper	
Enemies	

The below diagram shows the outcome through a stable mind. This is also an outcome when one's belief system is fertile due to pleasant past experiences. Hence, it impacts all the other layers with confidence and clarity; hence, the cycle moves toward success.

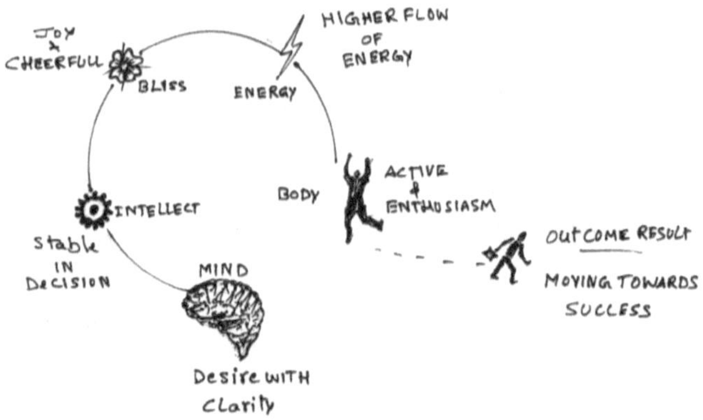

The Below Diagram shows the outcome through a fearful mind. When one's belief system is solidified with fear due to unpleasant past experiences, it impacts all the other layers and manifests in the form of fear, sadness, low energy, and laziness, and leads to failure, loss, or even depression.

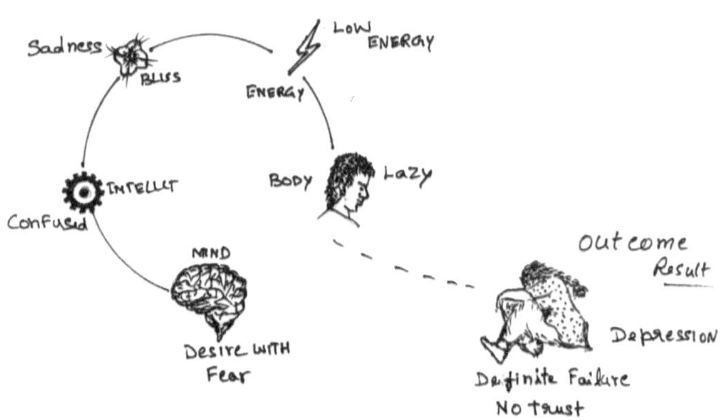

intellect:

Intellect is the faculty of reasoning, discernment, and judgment, allowing us to process information, make decisions, and differentiate between right and wrong. Intellect is the guiding force that evaluates choices and directs the body toward purposeful actions. It works in harmony with the mind, emotions, and body, ensuring that we lead a balanced, thoughtful, and fulfilling life.

Intellect plays a crucial role in existence, it is responsible for the selection or rejection of desires, distinguishing between good and bad, right and wrong. Spontaneous decisions regarding these desires are made by the intellect, based on past experiences and accumulated wisdom.

If a person operates from the stronger, positive side, then many large intentions which are meant to benefitmay take shape successfully. However, if the person has doubts, attachments, or a judgmental intellect, even the clearest wishes and intentions will not bear fruit.

For example, in cases of suicidal thoughts, if the mind suggests suicide but the intellect is stable, the act will not happen. The intellect, when stable, prevents harmful actions, regardless of what the mind suggests. This mechanism operates independently of the body.

Clarity and stability in mind and intellect are essential for achieving success. A clear wish, combined with unwavering intention and stability, ensures positive results. In contrast, doubts, emotional attachments, and confusion in the intellect hinder success, no matter how strong the desire is.

Job-Oriented and Business Mindsets:

Some job-oriented people are happy with their work, stable in their jobs, and satisfied with family life. Their vision is limited to maintaining this stability. However, due to fear, they often fail to dream bigger or take up a *Sankalp* (intention). Similarly, small-scale business owners hesitate to expand their businesses out of fear.

For example, city dwellers may wish to buy a house but opt for cheaper options in rural areas due to cost concerns. If one firmly decides, "I will buy a house in this specific area," and holds that intention steadily, it will manifest. People often believe that the first requirement to fulfill the desire is money, but a stable intention can attract the required money as a result.

It's important not to share your ideas with people unnecessarily, during gossip, or to seek attention.

The effects of different mindset on other layers (Koshas):

Mindset	Intelect	Bliss	Energy	Physical body Result
Calm	Nonjudgmental	Cheerful	Energetic	Active
Focused	Innovative	Joyful, timeless	Energetic	Active
Aggressive	Stubborn	Heaviness	Overflow	Reactive
Frustrated	Wrong decision	Helpless	Scatted	Reactive
Trauma	Emotional decision	Shrinking	Low	Lonely

This table indicates the results at different layers of existence depending on the state of mind.

Kaya, Vacha, Manasa:

Action, words and intention

A single energy reflects through three things:

Kaya, Vacha, Manasa

Action words and intention

However, usually, our words, actions, and intentions are different, and that is where the problem arises from.

For example, in the social world, people greet each other with love and respect but think maliciously and judge them behind their backs.

When your intention is not aligned with your words and actions or none of them is aligned with one another, it manifests as a curse, and if these three are tuned and reflected as one energy, it manifests as blessings.

In the social world, we cannot be like King Harishchandra, but aligning these three is also important; hence, in certain situations, we need to handle it very skillfully. We cannot exactly say the words we feel, but we can twist them to create a win-win situation with good intentions.

It is essential to analyze the category of different people and handle them accordingly.

For example, in the corporate world or any social networking, we need to first categorize people and then skillfully align our thoughts, words, and actions so that the alignment is not disturbed, and yet we can manage people of different categories.

Sankalpa - (Selfimagination)

So'kamayata, bahu syamprajayeyeti, satapo'tapyata, satapastaptva

idagmsarvamasrijatayadidamkinca,tatsrishtvat adevanupravishat

He (the Supreme Self) desired: "May I be many, may I be born. He performed austerities. Having performed austerities, He created all this— whatever there is. Having created all this, He entered into it. Having entered into it, He became both the manifested and the unmanifested, both the defined and undefined, both the supported and unsupported, the intelligent and the non— intelligent, both the real and the unreal.

(citation:https://www.esamskriti.com/e/ Spirituality/Upanishads-Commentary/Taittiriya- Upanishad~-Petal-8-1.aspx)

Sankalpa, derived from the Sanskrit words *Swa* (self) and *Kalpita* (imagination), represents a deliberate alignment of thought and energy towards a desired goal. This whole creation came into existencethrough divine intention that isself-imagination or **(Sankalpa)** of the Almighty.At present humans have invented advanced technologies and reachedother planets, all these inventions are because of somebody's *Sankalpa*. So, nothing is impossible, for every individualthe only thing is to have right clarity of *Sankalp* to achieve that goal.

Every desire is an imagination:

A *Sankalp* (resolution or intention for achieving a goal or desire) arises in the mind, but it is carried forward by a stable intellect. If the intellect is confused and doubtful, the *Sankalp* will not manifest effectively because confusion becomes the driving force. A stable intellect provides the clarity and determination necessary to push the *Sankalp* towards realization, ensuring that no obstacle can hinder its progress. Conversely, if negativity dominates, the same mechanism will lead to negative outcomes or failure.

When a *Sankalp* (intention) arises, such as a desire for a peaceful life, good relationships, or a successful business, its origin may be either an individual or divine (Brahman). In both cases, the outcome depends on whether the *Sankalp* is supported by a stronger (positive) side.

The intellect has freewill to choose between stability and doubt when supporting a *Sankalpa*. For instance, many lower-class or uneducated individuals often demonstrate a clear and stable intellect. Despite lacking financial resources, knowledge of business, or external support, their unwavering clarity about their goal places them on the positive side, leading to successful outcomes. Their limited options force them to concentrate entirely on their desires, fostering an unshakable belief in their potential and the clarity naturally instills discipline and drives them towards their goals. For example: Developing small businesses such as tea shops, paan shop etc.

In contrast, a highly educated individual with financial stability might have a strong Sankalpa, such as building a successful business or pursuing a big dream. Yet, if their goal and vision is clouded by doubt, distractions, or attachment to outcomes, their energy becomes fragmented. This lack of clarity weakens the Sankalpa's potency, creating barriers to manifestation.

This process explains how manifestation occurs, whether positive or negative. Having a *Sankalpa* is not inherently wrong, as creation itself began with a *Sankalpa*, and all maintenance in the universe operates through it. Scientifically also, a stable *Sankalpa* triggers neurochemical reactions, which in turn attract actions and reactions that lead to its fulfillment.

In today's world, many people live according to external expectations. Society often molds individuals into predesigned paths, leaving them feeling disconnected from their true desires. Yet, there are those who defy this flow; they are the visionaries, innovators, and leaders who actively shape their destinies with clarity and intention. These individuals don't leave their futures to chance. Instead, they harness the focused power of *Sankalpa* to create their reality.

It is a sacred vow, a binding commitment to oneself and the universe to manifest an intention. We explored the power of *Sankalpa*, the intentional alignment of thought and energy towards a desired goal. Sankalpa is the seed of every goal, the powerful intention that sets us into motion, and the forces that shape our reality.

Much like a tree that requires healthy roots to flourish. Our thoughts, emotions, and actions must be grounded in purity for our desires to manifest effectively. A tree can only grow as strong as its roots; similarly, the success of our Sankalpa is determined by the purity and clarity of the foundation from which it springs. Here, we will make an effort to transform the negative emotions residing in all the layers of our being, such as fear, doubt and confusion, into positive intentions, building strength and stability to take firm resolutions (sankalpa) and work towards achieving our goals.

Lack of harmony with the universe and non-alignment with our true self leads to obstacles in life, such as untruthful actions through body, wrong Vastu, negative presence in the home, cheating in business and work, ignorance in mind, incorrect decision-making, and relationship issues. Hence, our surroundings will attract the same experiences, people, and living. This disharmony, due to the lack of union in every aspect will create obstacles in the flow of the universe through us, which contributes towards destruction in all aspects and compromises success in life.

The obstacle is dark energy, and therefore, if we lack the below three transformative powers in life it will be followed by destruction, failure, disease, and death.

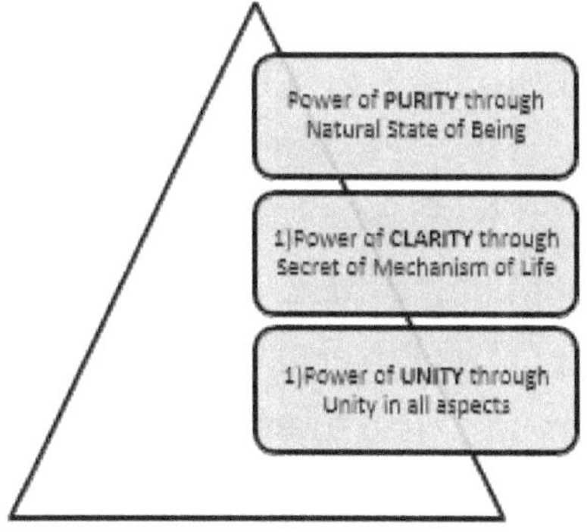

A positive, stable, strong, Sankalpa generates three transformative powers: (unity, purity, clarity)

1. Unity: Aligning the mind, body, and energy so they work together seamlessly.

2. Purity: Moving closer to a natural state of being, free from fear and doubt.

3. Clarity: Bringing a clear vision of your path forward, this allows for decisive actions.

The Ancient Wisdom of Sankalpa:

The concept of Sankalpa is deeply rooted in Indian spiritual traditions. In ancient practices, before any ritual or Pooja (prayer offering), it is customary to take a Sankalpa- an intention or vow aligning the individual's will with the divine flow of the universe. This act signifies planting the seed of desire into the cosmos, trusting in its natural progression and fulfillment. Unlike short term wishes, Sankalpa is a mindful commitment to align personal desires with the greater cosmic order. Ancient teachings emphasize unwavering faith in one's Sankalpa, trusting the divine timing of its manifestation despite challenges. When the intellect aligns with clarity and focus, it propels the Sankalpa forward with unwavering determination. In this state, no obstacle can deter the individual from achieving their goals.

A person has freewill, an ability to either support the stability of the Sankalpa or introduce doubt and uncertainty.

TYPE OF SANKALPA:

Whether individual or divine, **Sankalpa** is a resolve or intention that arises to manifest. There are different types of **Sankalpa**: one for maintaining the body (such as hunger or thirst), one for the family (to love, care, and provide for daily needs), and one for society (to ensure harmony and goodness). For example, if the body's **Sankalpa** is to drink water and one becomes too lazy to do so, dehydration will occur. Similarly, if the **Sankalpa** for family is to take care of their daily needs and one keeps on postponing it without stability, it creates chaos among family members. When one is on the negative side, they often expect others to bring positive results. However, they remain negative and act as if, they are positive. Many a times, one may have experienced failure on the negative side and accepted it. Now, one can choose to move to the positive side and observe the change. For instance, if the main switch is off, continuously pressing other buttons won't help— it's about addressing the core and the issues from the root."

There are many types of Sankalpa, some of them are listed below-:

a) **Individual Sankalpa-**
- **Natural Sankalpa**
- **Self-believedSankalpa**
- **Authoritative Sankalpa**

b) **Family Sankalpa**

c) **CollectiveSankalpa**

d) **Choice less Sankalpa**

Individual Sankalpa: Refers to a personal resolution or intention that is unique to an individual, addressing their specific needs, aspirations, or challenges. When one determines to walk the journey of Sankalpa alone, it becomes challenging, since people tend to demoralize and put them down rather than extending support.

Hence, after making a personal resolution, to progress smoothly in that resolution and reach the goal, it is important to avoid letting others know about it as much as possible".

Natural Individual Sankalpa: Sometimes, we deeply think about a desire and strongly wish for it to be fulfilled. Then, we forget about it. Here automatically seeding happened in nature, and after a long time we realize that wish is automatically fulfilled, even when we no longer need it. When it happens, we remember that we had once wished for it very deeply and had forgotten about it. When such a desire arises in the mind and is fulfilled after a long time, it means that nature itself brings that desire into our mind and fulfills it. Nature wanted this Sankalpa to manifest through us.

Self-believedSankalpa: One may not believe in the existence of God or nature, but he completely believes in himself, thinking, 'I will do it'& "I have to do it" (he is self-confident). Even in this case, nature supports him indirectly or invisibly, but he may not recognize it because his belief is solely in himself.

Some people have great belief in God, but they consider karma itself as God and give utmost importance to their actions. They move toward their goals with a very positive mindset, and nature fulfills their desires as well.

Some people have great trust in themselves, their actions, and God. They believe that if they perform good deeds with a positive mindset, God will surely fulfill their desires. Nature fulfills the desires of such people in the best possible way, and they also set an example for the world.

Authoritative Individual Sankalpa: SomeSankalpais such that they are made by one person but carried out by someone else. For example, in an office, a boss might have a Sankalpa to increase the company's profit. The resolution is of the boss, but due to his authority, employees must work on it, whether they are aligned or not. Sometimes, a few employees work on it with interest, while others do it unwillingly. The results might be fruitful, but it may not be as effective as it could have been.

If the boss, instead of imposing decisions, involve all the employees in decision making and collaboration, and encourages and aligns them with the company's goals, the outcome would be far superior.

Similarly, in a family, parents often impose their wish on children, pressuring them mentally to fulfill their aspirations. As a result, children may have to abandon their own dreams to meet their parents' expectations. This can lead to situations where children neither achieve their parents' goals nor feel free to pursue their own, potentially resulting in depression.

On the other hand, there are instances where children adopt their parents' aspirations as their own and strive to fulfill them successfully. Such Sankalpa, where the will of one is imposed on another, are referred to as **authoritative Sankalpa**.

Family Sankalpa: A **family Sankalpa** is a collective decision or agreement made by family members to address a specific goal, issue, or situation. It often involves collaboration, communication, and mutual understanding to ensure the well-being and harmony of the family.

Sometimes, an entire family comes together to make a decision that solves problems for everyone and helps achieve shared goals. For instance:

- When there is a wedding or any family function in the family, responsibilities are divided among the members, each person assigned with specific tasks.

- If the family is planning a picnic, everyone is given a role to ensure smooth coordination.

- When building a new house, tasks are distributed so that everyone contributes to the project.

- If someone is unwell in the family, different members take on various responsibilities to support and manage the situation.

Such collective efforts demonstrate teamwork, mutual support, and the importance of sharing responsibilities to overcome challenges and achieve family goals.

Collective Sankalpa: It is a Sankalpa or desire rising in the consciousness of a group of people together.

For Example: A similar pattern was observed in Indian middle-class families of the 1970s and 1980s. Owning a car seemed like an unattainable dream. It came out as collective Sankalpa arising in every home and after the 2000s, car ownership became a reality for many. These examples show that belief in one's Sankalpa is as important as the intention itself.

The below diagram shows the outcome of the unwavering mind and Sankalpa. Overcoming the initial struggle and manifesting.

How Sankalpa works on Kosha:

The **impacts of Sankalpa (intention or resolve)** on the koshas (layers of existence) are profound, as it works through all levels to align thoughts, energy, and actions with a higher purpose. Sankalpa is not just a mental resolution; it is a deeply transformative process that affects the physical, energetic, mental, intuitive, and blissful layers of the self.

Sankalpa (a positive intention or resolution) works deeply on the koshas by aligning all layers of existence with a focused purpose. A Sankalpa is not merely a goal; it is a heartfelt, affirmative resolve that arises from our deeper self. It activates transformation across all koshas, harmonizing the physical, mental, and spiritual aspects of our being.

Understanding the Root, is Essential for Achieving Your Goal:

Imagine a tree infected by insects or pests. The symptoms of infestation are visible in the branches and leaves, but the true problem lies at the roots. If the roots are neglected, no amount of pruning or care for the branches will save the tree. Similarly, in life, we often focus on the surface-level challenges (our actions, relationships, and external circumstances) without addressing the root causes of these issues. True transformation happens when we look inward and address the very core of our thoughts, emotions, and beliefs.

This realization reveals the core of the matter: we often fail to recognize the subtle ego, Ahankar, that drives the search. Ego (Ahankar) is the false self that believes in the need to search, to find, and to attain. But when we acknowledge that nothing external can truly define us, it begins to dissolve the hold of Ahankar and we enter the space of pure Beingness- a state that is untouched by external circumstances, free from the need for validation or discovery. It is from this space of inner perfection that true transformation begins.

When weembark on the journey of self-discovery, there is a tendency to focus on finding something "out there," a goal, or an identity that we can strive towards. But in truth, the search is not about finding anything external. The search for yourself is a paradox: when you believe you have something to find, the searcher remains. It is only when you realize there is nothing to search for, when you let go of the notion of searching altogether, then you are faced by the reality of your Beingness (your true, untouched self) and you will feel free from within. In this state of being free, one is allowing nature to flow and manifest of pre-decided divine desires, which are far better than our capabilities, and superior to what we wanted for us. This elevates us to such a high level where we can not only uplift ourselves, but also contribute to the welfare of others.

Fear:

Fear is not just an emotion; it is an energy that permeates the very fabric of our being. When we harbor fear at the root of our being, it seeps into every cell, affecting our thoughts, actions, and interactions with others. Fear shapes the way we perceive ourselves and the world around us, creating barriers to growth and manifestation. It clouds our judgment, limits our potential, and keeps us stuck in a cycle of self-doubt and limitation.

The best and most effective way to overcome fear is to face the thing we are afraid of with strength and determination. The key to overcoming fear is to address it at the root level. Rather than merely attempting to control or suppress fear, we must dissolve it at its source. Sometimes, complete dissolution may not be possible, but it is crucial to transform or channelize fear, so it no longer dominates our actions. Just as a tree absorbs nutrients that are beneficial for its growth, we must allow only the positive energies to nurture our roots, while channelizing or letting go off the negative ones, such as fear.

Doubt and confusion:

Shree Krishna said in Bhagwat Geeta: -
'Samshaya Atma Vinashyati',

"A person filled with doubt is destroyed."

This means that doubt is a harmful force which covers our soul and weakens the power of resolve. It silently undermines our intentions, breaking their foundation. When doubt takes hold, it creates a cycle of indecision, hesitation, and extreme fear.

A person plagued by doubt cannot take decisive action or have firm faith. This leads to indecision, fear, and ultimately failure to achieve goals, whether material or spiritual.

It emphasizes the importance of faith (in oneself, one's actions, or higher truths) as the foundation for success and growth.

A doubtful mind cannot hold a clear and focused Sankalpa. If doubt remains at the root, it will manifest in personal, professional, relational, and every other aspect of life. Actions driven by doubt are often performed in secrecy, not from a place of authenticity, and without full commitment. Doubt leads to a false sense of self, a dual personality that is disconnected from the true self. This misalignment creates friction in life, preventing smooth flow of energy necessary for manifestation.

Confusion is like gambling with decisions; it arises from the layer of intellect (Vigyanmaya Kosha) and is often unstable and unclear. The root of confusion lies in fear, and it is further influenced by both good and bad experiences, which can lead a person into the state of uncertainty.

Confusion arises from a lack of belief in oneself and in many other things. Most people, when faced with confusion, hesitate to act, step back from their work, or make poor decisions. A confused individual often struggles to trust their own judgment, which becomes their greatest weakness. This lack of self-belief causes them to rely on others' decisions; hence, the outcomes may sometimes be favorable or unfavorable.

Confusion is also a sign of a lack of confidence and courage. Without these qualities, one cannot achieve anything significant in life. Confusion allows weaknesses to take root, diminishing a person's ability to realize their full potential. Over time, it fosters a habit of constant compromise, leading one to accept less in life and settle for mediocrity.

Effort:

Example of Garuda Vidya- the eagle, a symbol of strength and majesty, offers us a profound lesson. When it begins its ascent from the earth, it needs to use tremendous energy, flying its wings against the pull of gravity. This initial effort is crucial – it allows the eagle to rise, overcoming resistance to reach its peak. The eagle no longer needs to flap its wings once it reaches a certain level in sky. It glides effortlessly for hours, soaring in circles with stability and grace, without putting in additional effort to stay in flight.

Similarly, when we set Sankalpa, our inner resolve, in the beginning we must put complete efforts to lift off and get entirely involve into the task, committed to overcoming the challenges we face, then at one level it will become effortless and supported by Universe.

The Impact of Negative Emotions on the Roots:

To better understand how negative emotions affect our lives, imagine there are three types of seeds: one strong, one weak, and one infected. The strong seed represents a clear, positive intention, free from doubt or fear. The weak seed symbolizes an intention clouded by uncertainty, but still capable of growth. The infected seed, however, symbolizes the root of negative emotions—fear, doubt, and unresolved trauma. Just as infected insects can destroy a tree by attacking its roots, a tree with healthy roots will only grow stronger. The tree growing through the stronger seed will give rise to healthy tree.

On the other hand, when the root contains fear, doubt, or negative energy, it becomes extremely difficult to take the right actions, take sound decisions, and attract supportive people. In fact, we may unknowingly attract people and situations who mirror our negative states, creating unhealthy relationships and toxic environments.

Perfecting the Roots:

The main part of a tree is its root. The root also spreads beneath the tree. Simply treating some infected branches of the tree, will not eliminate the infection from the root. The treatment must be applied to the entire root and ensure that the infection does not spread again. The roots must be treated repeatedly until the desired result is achieved.

On the other hand, when we perfect our roots, which means addressing and clearing out negativity, we create a foundation rooted in trust, belief, transparency, and self-confidence. From this space, our intentions are pure, our vision is clear, and our actions align with our truest desires. When we align with the purity of our inner being, we naturally attract the right people, opportunities, and circumstances to support our growth and manifestation.

This is the power of perfecting the roots; it is not merely about changing external circumstances, but about transforming the inner state of being. When we release the fear and doubt that once governed us, we allow the energy of clarity, purpose, and authenticity to flow freely, creating a life that reflects our true essence.

Yet again, when you are walking the journey of your goal, take a moment to reflect on the impressions or beliefs you are carrying about it—the ones you may not have noticed before. If you find fear, confusion, doubt, or other negative impressions, it indicates there is an *"infection in the root "*of your efforts. Understand, these unnoticed impressions might have influenced your behavior and working patterns with people and affected your progress till date.

If such negativity exists, we must address it immediately. Carrying negative emotions while working towards our goal will prevent us from reaching it. And even if we reach it, those unresolved negativities may pull us down again. It's essential to overcome these inner obstacles to achieve our goal with a sense of confidence and stability.

Hidden enemies:

Lack of harmony with the universe and non-alignment with our true self leads to obstacles in life, such as untruthful actions through body, wrong Vastu, negative presence in the home, cheating in business and work, ignorance in mind, incorrect decision-making, and relationship issues. Hence, our surroundings will attract the same experiences, people, and living. This disharmony, due to the lack of union in every aspect, will create obstacles in the flow of the universe through us, which contributes towards destruction in all aspects and compromises success in life.

The obstacle is dark energy, and therefore, if we lack the below three transformative powers in life it will be followed by destruction, failure, disease, and death.

These hidden enemies will never hinder a stable and clear inner state.

Stability and Clarity:

Staying committed in your **Sankalpa** (resolve or intention) requires a combination of mental clarity, emotional strength, and disciplined action.

Ensure your Sankalpa is specific, meaningful, and aligned with your core values. Write it down as a positive statement, e.g., "I have completed this project with dedication and focus. I am living it with every breadth and each step is towards my goal." And with awareness feed this in your consciousness and aura. Science is before anything, be it disease or desire, cultivates in our subtle body way before it is visible in our physical body.

The goal to achieve your Sankalpa is stability. Stability does not come from a constant effort to control or maintain Sankalpa, but from understanding and aligning with your true nature. When you are in tune with your thoughts and intuition, you no longer need to hold onto Sankalpa or forced stability. You live without fear, and with ease and clarity; your actions flow naturally from this space of alignment.

Just as a tree grows steadily when its roots are strong, we too can grow steadily and gracefully when we perfect the roots of our being. By addressing the core of our thoughts, emotions, and actions, we can create a life that is aligned with our deepest truth and purpose.

Sankalpa ToWards Manifestation

Deeply believing in and feeling passionate about your Sankalpa helps in its manifestation.

Regularly repeating the *Sankalpa*, especially during meditative states or at moments of focus, reinforces its presence in the subconscious mind.

Manifestation

Time has witnessed everything, from the birth of the universe to the rise of human civilizations, from the smallest atom to the vastest galaxies. In this infinite expanse, we humans stand out, capable of not just surviving but thriving, creating, and living meaningful lives.

"To avoid confusion in worldly life, one can always choose between two options: either decide a goal with a stable intellect or choose not to have a goal at all, so that one does not get stuck in between. On the other hand, one must examine if there is a subtle fear, such as, 'I don't want to set a goal, and I am comfortable with my current situation.' This fear will prevent one from stepping out of their comfort zone. A goal lacks power if one is unclear about it. Nature contributes to one's goal in many ways—through people, circumstances, situations, family, friends, and more. Nature is always in support of the individual; however, how much one manifest depends on one's alignment and harmony with existence. A combination of both 'understanding' and 'being 'enables one to live a fruitful and beautiful life.

In this chapter, I want to share my absolute realizations with you. Everything I have learned, from my personal and spiritual journey, has brought me to this moment where I can open these secrets of realizations with you.

This chapter is an attempt to share a small fragment of my learning, one that removes the illusions and reveals the secret of manifestation, the understanding till the core of all creation.

To move forward in life and achieve stable success, being extremely happy or extremely sad can both become obstacles? This is because, at times, we get carried away by happiness or lost in sorrow. I have risen above all these things because, in 2013, by the grace of God, I experienced a glimpse of oneness—a profound experience that lasted for 9 and a half hours. This experience transcended time and the body.

The joy and sorrow that come with fame and loss, victory and defeat, are all just vibrations—simply a part of life. We fail to understand these vibrations and often get swept away by them. However, we are stronger than these vibrations and beyond them. Experiencing that oneness makes life much easier, as neither joy nor sorrow can deeply touch us anymore. We won't lose sight of our goals and will continue moving towards them, no matter what comes our way.

Calculation of manifestation:

This chapter on the Calculation of Manifestation delves into how various factors inside us such as the clarity of our intellect, the purity of our thoughts, our energy levels, and our emotional state, combine and influence the manifestations we experience in the world. The framework I present here allows you to understand how these inner forces can either align to create success or misalign leading to failure. It is important to grasp this concept because in the grand scheme of understanding the human mechanism of success and failure, we are not simply reactive beings, but we have the power to shape our reality by consciously aligning our internal state with the desirable outcomes. When we understand how the energy within us translates into tangible results, we can take proactive steps to nurture success rather than fall into the trap of unconscious failure.

Manifestation Calculation Table:

The Key Numbers: +9 and -9

As we all know that 9 is a universal number, let's see the calculation with respect to all the aspects of life and how they contribute to this total of 9.

In the table below, we explore the different layers of being or life. It is important to understand that

bliss is not merely an emotion but a deeper layer of existence that transcends intellect. This layer, referred to as Bliss, encompasses both states of sadness and blissfulness, which can be observed and experienced at this profound level of existence.

MECHANISM OF LIFE	Positive (Strong)		Negative (Weak)	
	Characteristics	Value Point	Characteristics	Value Point
Bliss	Blissful State	2.25	Sadness	2.25
Intellect	Stable	2.25	Confused	2.25
Mind	Detached	2.25	Attached	2.25
Prana (Energy)	Energetic	2.25	Low energy	2.25
Physical (food) body	Result: Healthy	9	Result: Illness	9

Assuming here that +9 is a Success number on positive side and -9 is a failure number on negative side. Suppose we give 2.25 to each complete function on both sides. So, if every aspect is complete (2.25) on positive side then the total will become 9 a success number. And, if you have 9 on the negative side it will go to failure.

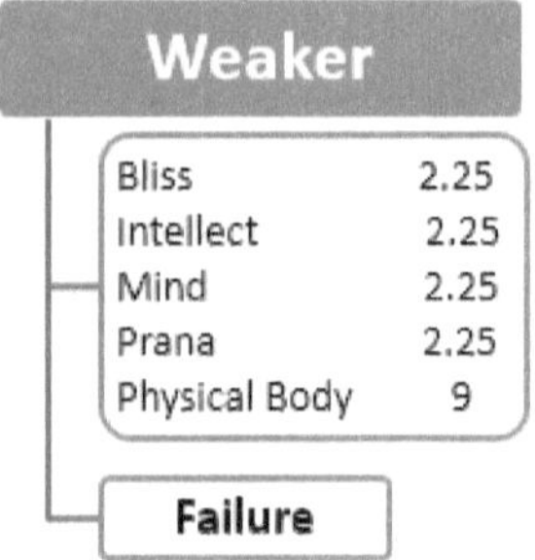

By looking at this calculation chart, you can calculate yourself whether your result on the stronger, weaker or mixed side.

Result of Negative and Failure Manifestation at different layers:

Manifestation Layer	Negative Impact/ Condition
Bliss (Anandmaya)	Surrounded by dark vibrations, lazy and lack motivation.
Intellect (Vigyanmaya)	Focused only on negativity, confused, distracted, and doubtful
Mind (Manomaya)	Driven by jealousy, resentment, hatred (particularly towards those who succeed), attached to fear and doubts, and unstable
Energy (Pranamaya)	Drives dark and negative actions, low and drained energy
Physical body (Arnamaya)	Unhealthy driven by illness, inactive and sluggish

Result of Positive and Success Manifestation at different layers:

Manifestation Layer	Impact/ Condition
Bliss (Anandmaya)	Enthusiasm and excitement to live
Intellect (Vigyanmaya)	Clear, focused, strong and unwavering intelligence
Mind (Manomaya)	Balanced and stable, well defined fearless goals
Energy (Pranamaya)	High energy and vitality
Physical body (Arnamaya)	Active

For Example: Below diagram shows thoughts of confused and negative mind set before beginning a startup; hence, attracting negative and failed manifestation

A person may be unaware of their confusions and beliefs. They often become stagnant due to their own self-imposed barriers, and unknowingly fall victim to these conditioned limitations. These inner barriers prevent them from taking steps forward. If this continues, their startup ideas will remain unfulfilled dreams.

However, if a person can encourage oneself by adopting a mindset free from choices that are influenced by these barriers, they can begin to explore and move forward. They can study how other companies started similar businesses, identify the skills they need to learn, determine the type of supportive team members required, and anticipate the challenges they may face. Preparing a comprehensive plan or report on their startup is crucial before taking the first step towards making their vision a reality.

All successful businessmen began their journey with failures, closing multiple ventures along the way. However, they learned valuable lessons from each failure and eventually returned with superior business models that established their dominance in that field. For Example: Dhirubhai Ambani attempted many failed businesses before the establishment of one of the world's largest industries. He always lived with high standards and accompanied those who reflected the same, even before he reached the heights he was determined to.

In the above example, let us see different patterns through diagrams representing the interconnection between mind set, relationships, business, health and the resultant outcome:

The below diagram represents the quality of relationships (the ups (Strong) and the downs (Weak)) resulting in one's life (business or family) due to the conditioned and confused mind set.

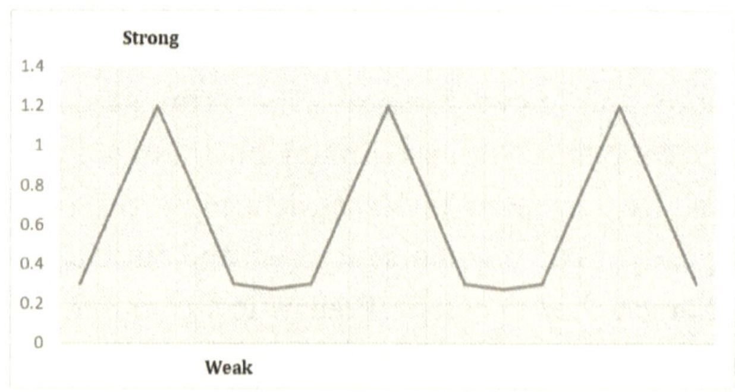

Often, when relationships are guided by a confused intellect, doubt arises towards business partners, employees and family members. This doubt attracts certain patterns of thoughts which will disrupt harmony in all the relationships around us, leading to instability and fluctuation, ups and downs.

Business with Confused Intellect and Attached Mind, starts strong but drops at later stages becoming weaker and weaker.

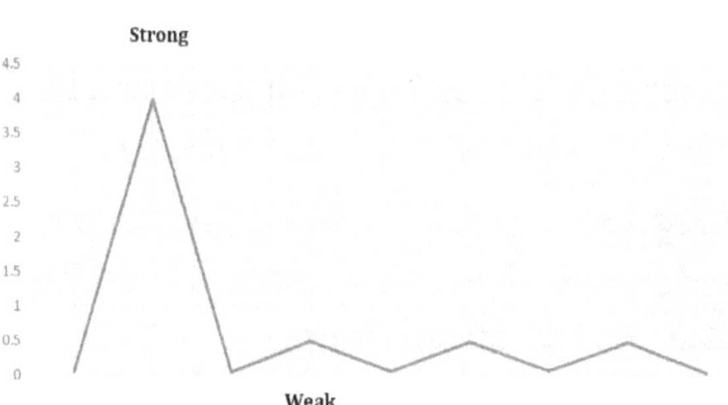

One may start a business with an initial investment and full of enthusiasm, but when the intellect is confused and the mind is overly attached, it will attract fear and insecurity in all decisions. This fear prevents clarity, stability, and patience, ultimately leading to losses in business due to poor decisions.

Business &Relationship with Stable Mind and Intellect, may start a little weak with challenges and questions but grow strong and run towards stability.

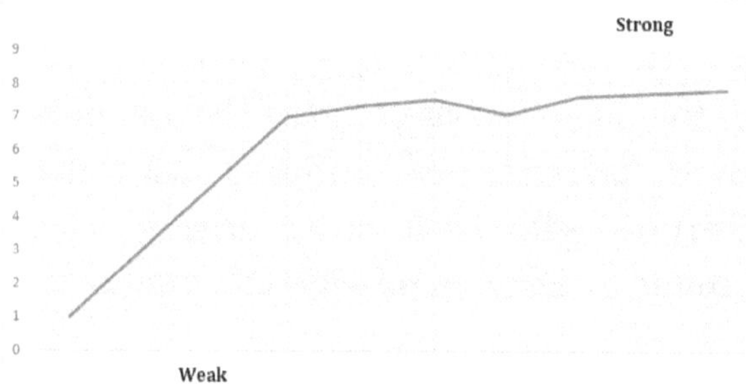

This diagram shows trust, growth, and success. Nature is always manifesting and providing, whether positively or negatively, what people truly need is unshakable faith—faith in nature, in God, and in oneself. Those who love their work deeply and remain unconcerned about outcomes or rewards often find that life flows smoothly and harmoniously.

Every aspect of life is interconnected; hence the below diagram shows how confused intellect and stressful mind set affects health.

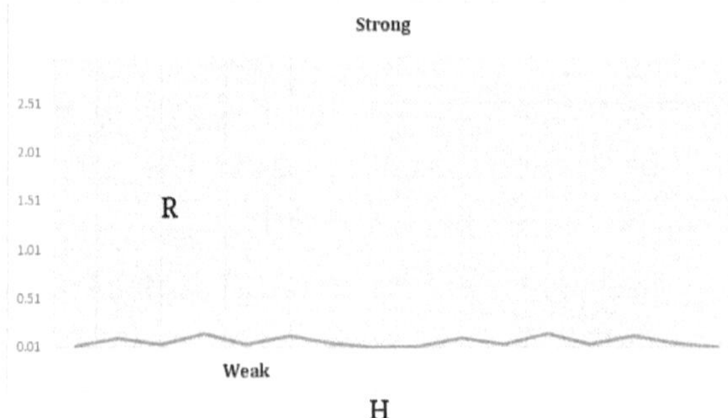

Confusion and fear can make a person lazy and inactive, eventually leading to wrong way of living, it follows illness in the body due to stagnation in life. Life graph tends to be on the weaker side and struggles to rise up towards stronger side.

In the same example, the below diagrams represent behavior of different attributes in coordination with each other arising from the background of different mindset and intellect:

Health Vs Relationship with Confused Intellect

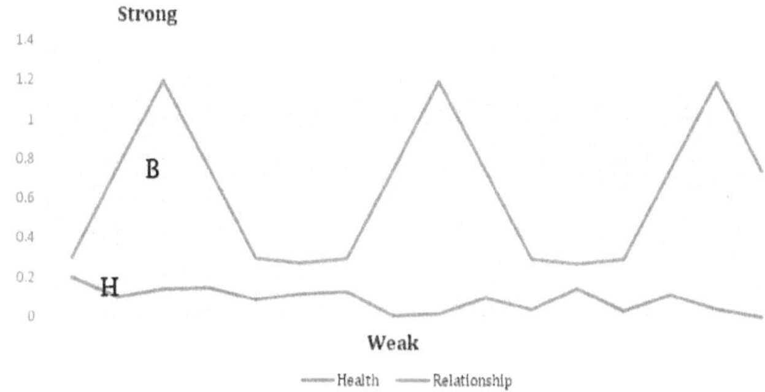

The impact of negative inner subtle layers affects health, often leading to illness, and causes instability in relationships, resulting in ups and downs.

Health Vs Business with Confused Intellect

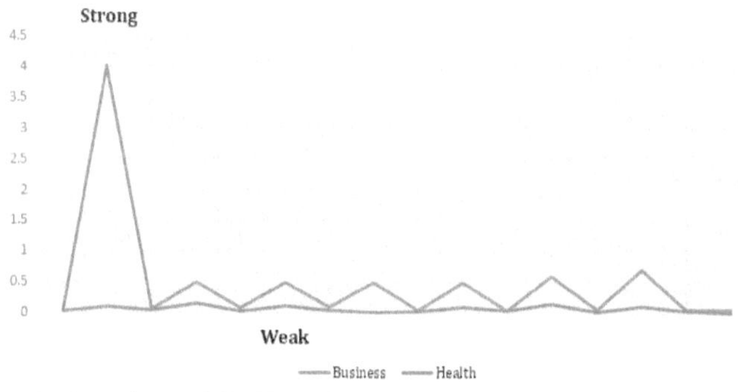

Health is influenced by all the negative aspects because the body and the world are reflections of what you carry within yourself. For the body, relationships, business, family, finances, and other areas of life are not separate entities; at a subtle level, whatever exists within you is expressed through your body and the world.

The body does not inherently understand concepts like wandering for enjoyment, spirituality versus materialism, success or failure, family, or business. The results in all aspects of life are expressed through the body; but occur from the world operating under this mechanism.

Bliss may not be in your control, but everything else is in your hands. The mind will continuously generate desires based on what it perceives, raising a desire for whatever it sees.

Whatever desire arises is carried forward either with stability or confusion. As the saying goes, "One says it but doesn't do it," because when there is doubt, you lack the energy to act. With confusion at every step, failure becomes inevitable.

Whether one is aware of it or not, the mechanism is already functioning through this body. Nature doesn't discriminate between various concepts such as good or bad, success or failure, or right or wrong— these are all part of the universe. However, it is up to the individual to decide what they want and how they want to shape their life, because humans have free will to choose and act.

Different Cycles of Manifestation:

Hence, depending upon the understanding and the time when one understands this mechanism, different cycles are attracted in one's life journey.

The below diagrams explain all different types of cycle manifested by different individuals as per their understanding of this mechanism described in this book.

a) Diagram of Manifestation:

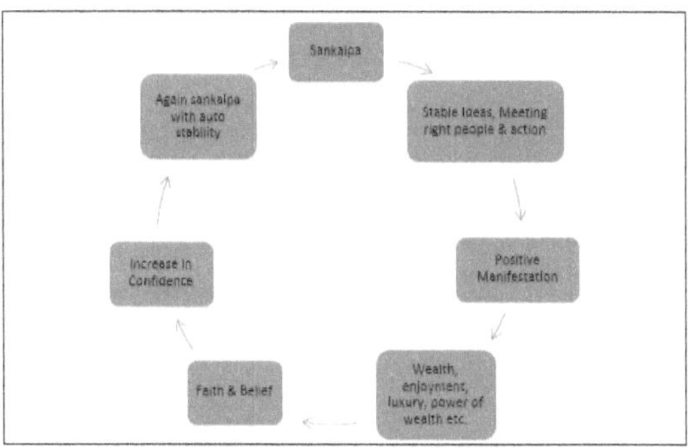

ASankalpa (intention) brings positive results like wealth, health, luxury, and power, it strengthens a person's faith in the divine and self. This confidence makes the future *Sankalpa* naturally stable, because the person begins to trust one's abilities. A stable individual values their *Sankalpa*.

For example, some teachers or astrologers excel at giving advice, and their students often achieve great success. However, these advisors' belief system and Sankalpa emphasize stability and an intention to support others. Hence, their life fostered, maybe not financially because their focus was not money.

However, overconfidence after success can lead to losing this value. It may result in unnatural behavior, disrupt future outcomes, and negatively affect personal life.

For example, many masters with numerous followers succeeded because their teaching methodologies and goals were very clear, which allowed their work to manifest effectively. However, their teachings often lose impact after they pass away. In case, if their followers continue to uphold and carry forward their intentions, the results can remain strong and impactful.

b) **Diagram of Failure:**

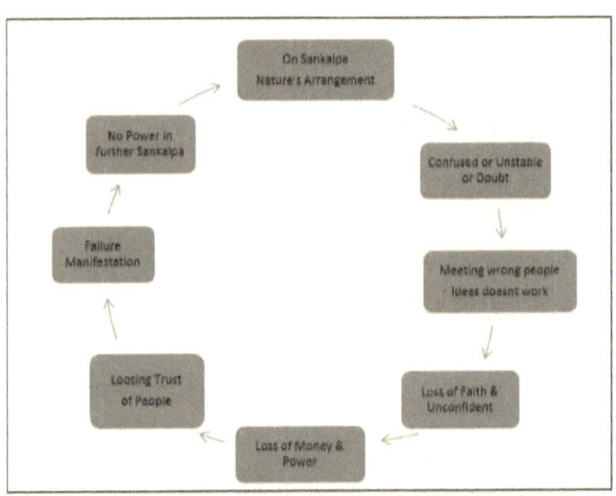

This failure manifestation starts with a **Sankalpa** (intention) that is unclear or unstable, which disturbs the natural flow of support around us. This lack of stability creates confusion, doubt, and emotional ups and downs. As a result, people may make poor decisions or connect with the wrong people.

When these mistakes lead to more failures, frustration grows, and the person becomes attached to their past failures. This attachment weakens their faith and confidence. Over time, one may lose important resources like money and power. This further reduces trust in oneself and others, creating a repeating cycle of failure.

In short, unclear intentions can lead to a chain of problems that feed into each other, making it hard to break free.

c) **Diagram of successful business cycle:**

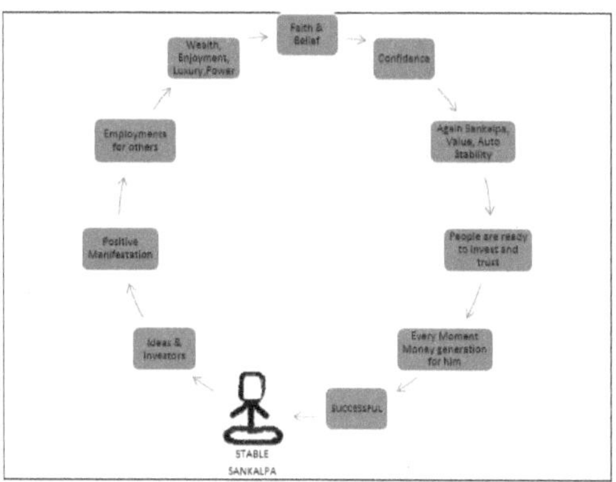

The diagram illustrates a continuous cycle of success, where each stage builds upon the previous one, creating a self-sustaining flow of prosperity. It begins with the human body, the source of ideas and intentions, which leads to the attraction of investors and the manifestation of positive outcomes. These outcomes result in employment opportunities, bringing wealth, enjoyment, luxury, and power. As success grows, faith and belief in the process strengthens, boosting confidence and reinforcing one's ability to manifest further achievements. This heightened confidence fuels Sankalpa (intention), aligning with personal values and creating a state of auto stability. As trust and investment from others follow, every moment becomes a money-generating opportunity, ultimately leading to greater success. The cycle then returns to the human body, where new ideas and intentions arise, continuing the loop of growth and success. This diagram captures the dynamic, ongoing nature of success, highlighting how each step feeds into the next, creating a perpetual cycle of manifestation and achievement.

d) Digram of success after failure:

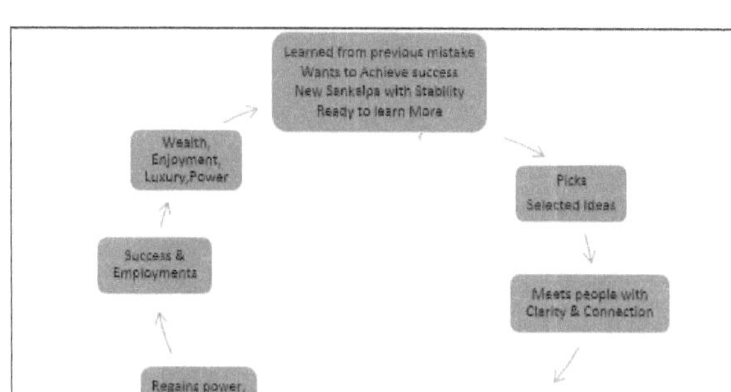

This diagram shows how failure can lead to success when people learn from their mistakes and set clear goals. It starts with someone reflecting on their past experiences and creating a new, strong intention (**Sankalpa**) with a willingness to learn.

They focus on clear ideas and build connections with the right people, which helps strengthen their vision and direction. With faith in their journey, they stay calm and steady even while facing challenges.

As they continue, positive results start to appear. They regain confidence, power, and trust. This success brings benefits like better job opportunities, more wealth, enjoyment, luxury, and influence.

In simple terms, learning from mistakes and having a clear plan can turn failure into lasting success.

e) **Digram of failure after success:**

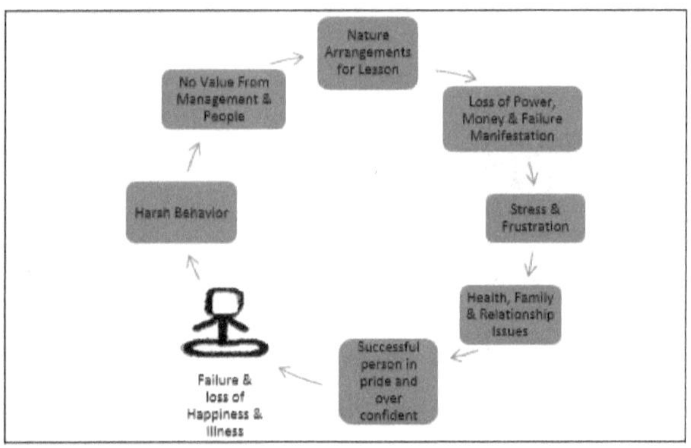

This diagram explains how failure can happen after success, focusing on the effects of pride and overconfidence. It starts when successful people become proud and overly confident. This attitude causes them to lose happiness and may even lead to illness.

With this negative mindset, they may start behaving harshly towards others, making people around them, including colleagues and management, value them less. As a result, life or nature creates situations to teach them a lesson. This often leads to losing power, money, and eventually experiencing failure.

As stress increases, their health, family, and relationships suffer, further damaging their success. In simple terms, pride and overconfidence can trigger a chain reaction that turns success into failure.

f) Diagram of Success after Success:

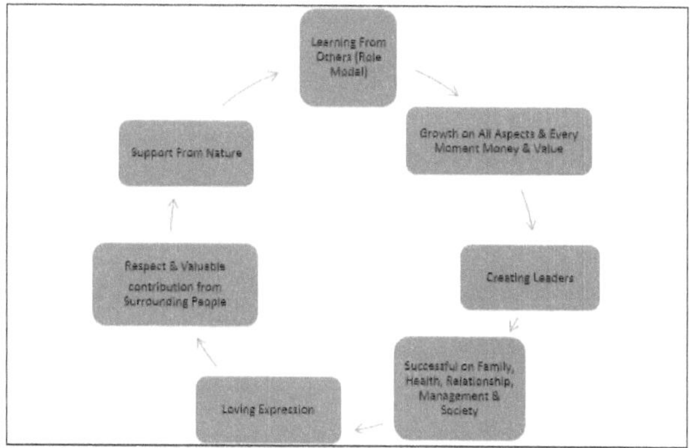

This diagram shows how success can grow continuously when it is built on positive qualities and actions. It starts with a person who is happy, kind, and successful, sharing positive energy and achieving good results.

Their kindness and success earn them respect and support from others. With help from nature and guidance from inspiring role models, they keep learning and improving. Their success spreads to different parts of their life—personal, professional, and financial.

As they grow, they also help others become leaders, which increases their positive influence. This ongoing cycle of success benefits everything in their life, including their family, health, relationships, work, and society.

In simple terms, being positive and kind leads to lasting success that grows and helps others too.

YOG, YOGYATA AND AYUSHYA:

In life, three essential forces govern our ability to manifest success: **Yog** (the right timing), **Yogyata** (readiness or eligibility), and **Ayushya** (physical capacity or vitality). To achieve success, all three factors are essential.

If one has an opportune moment but lacks the skills, eligibility, or physical strength to seize the opportunity, success may remain out of reach. Each of these forces must work in harmony, as relying solely on one without the others will naturally hinder the fulfillment of one's goals.

Ex: If a woman takes too long to decide about getting married, she might risk losing her **Ayushya** (vitality or energy) in terms of bodies ecology and, eventually, miss the perfect time (**Yog**) and eligibility (**Yogyata**) for the marriage.

Every individual has an optimal time for major life decisions. It is important to decide **now** what you truly want and remain stable in your decision. Align yourself with the stronger, more positive aspects of life.

Do not develop the habit of postponing tasks. Complete all your decided tasks in the present moment, and don't procrastinate. When you postpone, the supportive energies or subtle beings (called Angels, Rishis, Gods & Goddesses) present around you NOW (perfect YOG for YOU) may not be available when you choose to do the task later. Consequently, the results may not be fruitful because the supportive subtle energies may no longer align with the delayed timing.

When nature places you in a situation to learn and perform a task honestly, the angels and subtle beings around you will provide innovative ideas and support. Take full advantage of this opportunity, as these divine energies are pleased with your honesty and dedication.

However, if you postpone this opportunity, you risk disrespecting the angels and the subtle beings supporting you. At the very least, engage in some form of related work to honor their presence and assistance. By doing so, you show respect towards the divine forces helping you. Remember, do not delay—act NOW.

YATHA DRISHTI TATHA SHRISHTI -: "As your vision, so is your creation" or **"The world is as you perceive it."**This means that one only creates what one sees, perceives, and focuses on. A person has the power to create what they envision. Seeing refers to wishing, imagining, remembering a goal, and working towards it. If someone sees themselves in a certain place or with specific qualities and achievements, they will manifest those things in their life.

YATHA BHAVA TATHA BHAVATHI-: "As you think and feel(or attitude), so you become" or **"Your inner state determines your outer reality."**Whatever strong feelings one carries, it manifests—whether it is positive or negative, in any area of life.

YATHA PINDE TATHA BRAHMAMDE-:"As is the microcosm, so is the macrocosm" or **"As is the individual body, so is the universe."**Whatever is present in the seeds or cells of a person, the universe responds in the same way. If one carries emotions like hatred, jealousy, anger, or pride, their body cells will reflect these qualities, and the universe will mirror them through people, situations, and surroundings. As a result, the person loses their smile, the celebration of life, and the enjoyment of the present moment.

Mirror Effect of Universe

Persons Quality

Jealous
Lust
Tired
Lazy
Anger
Greed
Ego
Pride
Enemity
Hatred
Expects

Mirror Effect of Universe

Persons Quality

Loving
Helping
Sharing
Humorous
Committed

Manifestation Behavior:

You must avoid distractions and unhelpful relationships. To achieve a goal, your actions and interactions with others matter greatly. Maintaining silence means staying focused and avoiding unnecessary distractions or conflicts. Treating people surrounding you well, whether personally or professionally, fosters a positive and productive environment. For example, in a professional setup, respecting juniors shows humility and positive leadership qualities, while respecting seniors reflects an acknowledgment of their experience and wisdom. Together, these behaviors contribute to personal growth and success in achieving your goals.

The power of circle: Your circle of people is crucial in shaping your mindset and influencing your path. If you associate with those who focus on emotional blaming, negativity, or destructive habits like addiction or gambling, it can pull you into a toxic cycle and hinder your growth. However, surrounding yourself with polite and ambitious individuals, who value success and positivity, can inspire you to improve and align through and with their energy. So, if we are exceptional and humble in our approach, we will attract others towards our way of working and living; hence this is vice versa. People will admire our special qualities, learn from our example, and support our vision. Ultimately, this will help us build a strong, respectful, and motivated team or family that works harmoniously toward our goals while showing gratitude and loyalty.

Avoiding complaints fosters self-discipline and positivity, which are key aspects of **Tapasya** or focused effort. By avoiding negativity, we create an environment that naturally attracts individuals who align with our vision and values. We must spend time only with those who relate to our mission, purpose and energy. By doing so, we ensure that our energy is channeled effectively and in tune with our environment, fully supporting our growth and success. It will in turn help attract the right people to form a supportive and harmonious team for achieving your goal.

Every day, one should reflect on oneself and work on improving one's behavior, character, and personality. By identifying their emotional patterns—whether they exhibit fear, anger, frustration, positivity, or negativity—and their body language, individuals can make conscious efforts to improve. It's important to remain aware of one's inner state and habits, as these influence how others perceive them. Especially for someone aspiring to become a successful businessman, maintaining a positive as well as a professional character is crucial. For example, if we want money for our business and we approach a highly successful and rich businessman. However, these people always do proper research on one's background before engaging in them or investing in their business. Thus, to attract such investors, we need to consistently refine our character and behavior and build a strong and positive reputation. It is very essential.

There are many influential and wealthy individuals in the world, such as spiritual leaders, politicians, businessmen, motivational speakers, and teachers. They often speak inspiring words but do not practice the behavior they preach or act according to their teachings. As a result, over time, they gradually lose their value. Their core members may conspire against them since they might know their reality and secrets.

Golden and Dark manifestation (golden clarity): Golden thinking refers to the clear and stable mindset that leads to success, whereas dark thinking refers to negative accumulation, which is harmful and leads to failure.

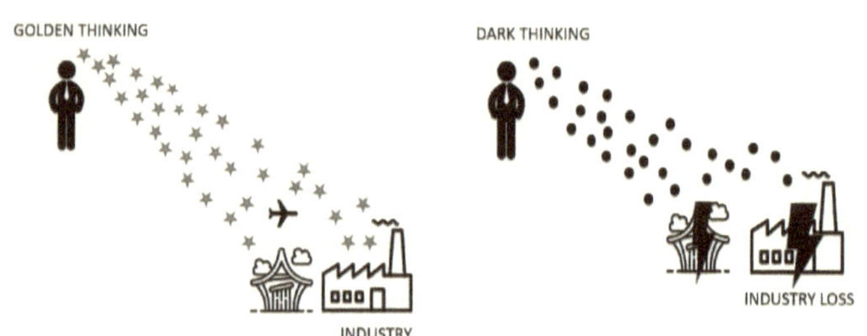

Therefore, since we cannot change everyone around us, it is essential to focus on transforming ourselves from within and improving our behavior. If we feel we need some powerful external support to understand, implement, and transform and will be able to achieve it in a better way through someone's support, then there are numerous retreats and workshops for self-improvement, which we can attend and grab all powerful techniques and tactics to transform and success.

Value for time and energy:

Time waits for no one. Each moment wasted is a missed opportunity to take one step closer to your dream. To align with success, treat your time and energy as sacred. Prioritize your goals, eliminate distractions, and commit to the actions that push you forward.

Remember, every small step matters and every small step contributes towards your goal whether directly or indirectly—much like the eagle's graceful glide, which covers great distances without unnecessary effort.

The most powerful part of action lies in the present moment. One cannot do the action in the past or future, but what you do now shapes the future. The decisions you make today may seem small, but they create ripples that will expand into your tomorrow. This moment is the key to your future.

It is easy to think that there is always time to act later, to wait for the "right moment", but the truth is that **NOW** (Prati Pravesh means this moment) is the right moment. Every thought, every action, no matter how small, contributes to the unfolding of your life. The road you walk today leads to the destination you will reach tomorrow.

If you stop acting because you're worried about whether the outcome will be good or bad, the results can be very negative. During unfavorable planetary periods, things may become much worse, and even during favorable planetary periods, you may not get good results if you haven't acted. By not wasting the present moment and continuing to perform your karma, learning and improving constantly, a person can avoid severe difficulties even during weak planetary periods. They keep moving towards their goal. And by doing this consistently, when the planetary position becomes highly favorable, he will reach peak of success and that's the mechanism of success.

How to overcome from all the obstacles:

If you know how to control yourself then you are a master. I am not here to push you to change yourself; the power to improve your life—be it health, business, relationships, or mental well-being—is only in your hands. Now is the time to return to the source, as the world is in a state where most people, whether successful business owners or ordinary individuals, are under stress. Many cannot find ways to manage their stress. This is the moment to pause—not from responsibilities, but from the negative mindset that affects every aspect of life as well as our surroundings.

If you want to achieve success in life, don't dwell on the failure but focus on understanding why it happened. Identify the causes of the failure, analyze the underlying mechanism, challenge and change limiting beliefs, learn from the experience, and develop a clear plan to move forward.

There is no need to discuss or explain your failure to anyone. Instead, accept your situation, study, and focus solely on improving and growing yourself.

Do you want nature to teach you a lesson, or will you be prepared in advance by learning what is necessary?

When nature forces you to learn through challenging situations, it can be extremely difficult because nature doesn't compromise when it wants to teach a lesson. However, if you proactively learn by observing others' experiences, mistakes, and failures, and by using your own intelligence to make the necessary changes to your personality, nature will be pleased to support you and guide you toward success.

For example:-

1. During the COVID-19 pandemic, People went through a lot of suffering, but nature continued its work. Nature seemed to "heal" or rejuvenate in several ways like human activities slowed down due to lockdowns and restrictions:-

    •   With reduced industrial emissions and fewer vehicles on the road, air quality in many cities worldwide significantly improved. Levels of harmful pollutants dropped drastically.

    •   Many Rivers and lakes saw visible improvements in water quality. For example, the "Ganges" in India became noticeably clearer during the lockdown.

        If we don't keep nature clean then nature will clean itself which will be very difficult for us.

2. **Addictions:-** Like any addictions become extreme are affect your health, mental condition and surrounding. That time you will get warning advice from family members or doctors, getting warning by illness and also loosing ability of mental health. After receiving different types of warning signs, if you improve yourselves, you can set an example.

But if you don't, you move toward serious illnesses, which could even lead to death.

Always be ready to learn and keep learning.

Factors for Successful Manifestation:

- **Alignment**: All koshas must work in harmony. Imbalances in any kosha can block or distort the manifestation process. For example,a lack of energy (Pranamaya) or unclear intentions (Manomaya) may hinder progress.

- **Spiritual Connection**: Desires rooted in the Anandamaya Kosha (bliss body) are more likely to bring lasting happiness.

- **Practical Action**: The Annamaya Kosha (Physical body) must be engaged to turn ideas into reality.

Practices to Enhance Manifestation:

1. **Annamaya**: Physical fitness, proper diet, and rest.

2. **Pranamaya**: Pranayama, yoga, and energy-balancing practices.

3. **Manomaya**: Meditation, positive thinking, and emotional regulation.

4. **Vijnanamaya**: Self-reflection, goal setting, and ethical living.

5. **Anandamaya**: Gratitude, spiritual practices, and connecting with higher consciousness.

This mechanism is designed to help you understand rather than to confuse or overwhelm you. There's no need to rush into overcoming everything all at once. Instead, focus on making small, simple changes to your daily routine with awareness. You will naturally begin to notice the difference and move toward a more positive mindset and success. Remember, there's no need to exert excessive effort—this process should feel effortless.

When one becomes attached at every stage, it will be like a pendulum, swinging back and forth.

Faith and Beingness:

People who are deeply spiritual or are in *beingness* often think, "I don't want anything," and their lives manifest accordingly. For example, if someone believes "I need only food to survive", then nature will provide only food.

Sometimes, power or wisdom comes to a person without any conscious *Sankalpa*. This happens when nature intends to grant these abilities for the greater good. For example, some spiritual beings do not ask for anything, yet they naturally acquire powers that benefit others. Such wisdom flows with intelligence, creativity, freedom, and spontaneity.

Whether a *Sankalpa* arises from an individual or nature, all manifestations occur through intention. A person's current situation—financial, personal, professional, or health-related—reflects from their lifestyle and intentions.

If someone wants to improve their circumstances, they must take a clear *Sankalpa* aligned with how they wish to live. With faith, they will experience the manifestation power of nature.

Security and Faith:

We think that job-oriented individuals might be feeling secure because they have fixed jobs and salaries. However, this sense of security is superficial; internally they may still worry about their future and family. What they lack is faith—in nature, God, or themselves.

Nature already manifests and provides everything (positive or negative). One only needs to have faith. Complete faith in nature, God, or oneself can bring peace and confidence.

Some people love their work and do it dedicatedly without worrying about the returns or results. Their lives flow smoothly, illustrating the power of faith and alignment with natural rhythms.

Simple way to achieve success:

There are many ways one can set work pattern and practice to achieve goals with the help of universal support by understanding the life mechanism start your journey with following steps:-

a) Purifying or clearing all past believed fears and stubbornness about your goal.

b) Have sankalpa (set new or modified goal).

c) Well planned, be specific and clear mind set on goal and vision (feel the result during practice of manifestation techniques)

d) Learn more and collect valuable information about your goal and find the best way.

e) Contribute every steps positively and discuss only with related persons throughout the journey (maintain silence and behavior).

f) Readiness to face challenges on journey does not hesitate to take risk. (Do not stuck with the fear of failure)

g) Set target again and again (utilize the valuable time)

h) Work action, planning, and meetings only from externaly but from within yourself rest and relax and handover to universe or god from within see that slowly your journey towards goal will be in auto mode.

When you grow with the consistence habit of walking positively by understanding life mechanism with clarity on your journey of goal then automatically unseen layers (kosha) will be align with themselves. When they are align their is purity, this purity will attract pure universal flow. See that you will start receiving support from universe towards manifestation of your goal even you may get many failures but at the end you will reach your success on universal time that will be best time for you and all.

Practical Techniques of Manifestation And Retreats

Our conditioned mind (here we will say brain to whom the mind gives command) can transform and perceive knowledge through three different languages:

1. Reading: Gaining knowledge

2. Audio or Video: Listening and watching

3. Action: Self-practice and indulge in powerful transformative techniques.

The most significant transformation comes through action, when one performs certain techniques to make things effortless and easy.

Our conditioned brain is affected deeply; hence, healing and repairing are required. For example, a person is interacting happily and normally at one point in time, but at another, we hear them committing suicide; this is because the condition and behavior of the brain are unknown and unpredictable at times.

The condition of the brain is invisible. Everyone wants to come on the positive side, but our way of living and stress accumulation has adulterated our core. Therefore, healing and personal recreational retreats with experts are required.

Here are two effective and easy techniques that you can practice gaining insight into overcoming negative traits, implementing these mechanisms and manifesting your desires effortlessly in your life.

Water Manifestation:

The physical body contains a high percentage of water, and water cells are the first to absorb vibrations from the surrounding environment. The brain, which also has significant water content, is particularly affected. For example, stress damages brain cells first, which then impacts the nervous system and other organs.

**Steps for Water Manifestation: **

This practice should be carried out continuously for a minimum of 15 days, and you can extend it if desired.

**Schedule: **

Begin on the day after Amavasya (new moon) and continue until Purnima (full moon), a total of 15 days every month. Because moon represent water aliments.

**Procedure: **

1.   Take a glass of water.

2.   Visualize yourself living your desire.

3.   Clearly recite your desire to the water.

4.   Drink the water.

**Rules for Desires: **

1.   Your desire must be specific and time bound.

2.   Repeat the exact same sentence for all 15 days.

3.   Perform the practice just once each day.

4.   You can recite more than one desire but ensure that each one follows the above rules.

5.   On the last day (full moon), repeat the practice three times a day.

By following these guidelines, you can effectively harness the power of intention with water manifestation.

MURDHINI PRANA TECHNIQUE:

Attention and focus cannot be directed through just any part of the body; they can only be centered in the forehead area. This is due to the presence of Murdhini prana, located right behind the crest of the head (which is where the pandits traditionally keep their Shikha).

Attention arises solely from Murdhini prana, which transmits our desires forward for manifestation. Regardless of whether these desires are stable, confused, or mixed, complete attention to them emerges from Murdhini prana. The quality of the desire determines how prana can attract situations for its manifestation.

Prana is the life force energy that sustains the body. Our physical existence relies on prana, which encompasses five primary pranas and additional Upapranas. The entire Panchakosha—intelligence, memory, age, body structure, body type, behavior, balance, and movement—are all regulated by this prana.

To understand the technique, we first need to know the function of Murdhini Prana. This energy operates automatically, meaning that our attention and observation occur without conscious effort through Murdhini Prana. For instance, there are times when our eyes are fixed on something, yet we're actually lost in our thoughts and not truly seeing it; at this time also the observation is happening through Murdhini prana.

We often fail to notice the sensations and vibrations of negative emotions and feelings that arise within us. These vibrations move from the navel to the throat, and negative sensations can release harmful chemicals in our bodies which drives our reaction. However, if we can observe these feelings, emotions and their sensations, they will dissipate. This understanding forms the basis of the Murdhini Prana Technique.

The technique involves consciously sitting and observing our emotions. While Murdhini prana is always observing, we bring to the forefront the negative emotions and patterns we carry, such as anger, jealousy, and hatred. By doing this, we bring these feelings under the attention of Murdhini, which helps diminish their power. This delicate act of observation assists in releasing them.

For example, if a thief is attempting to steal when someone is watching, he is unlikely to succeed. Similarly, when we consciously observe our emotions, thoughts, and feelings, it registers with Murdhini Prana. Practicing this daily can ultimately free us from these negative influences. This process enhances our capacity for observation. The more we consciously observe, the more we transform reactions into thoughtful responses.

Learning Advanced Techniques for remarkable results:

There are many powerful Techniques to Manifest one's Sankalpa to achieve success. There are many powerful ancient methods to achieve what you want in your life. Ancient manifestation techniques through nadi, self, planet, tree, and angels but this can only be passed on in physical presence.

There are also numerous techniques to overcome negative traits and release strong impressions that hold us back from excelling.

In order to learn advanced and highly impactful techniques and undergo deep-rooted cleansing, there are recreational retreats conducted by Life Mechanism Consultancy, and the facilitator will be K. Krishnanand, the author of the book. Contact details for the same are provided at the back of the book.

Let's experience, learn, educate, grow and share.........

Upcoming book of K. Krishnananda

The Hidden Keys to Sustainable Success Success is more than external achievements—it is about aligning with the universal flow of life. Your position today results from past choices, but your future depends on self-awareness and a clear vision. When you set a strong Sankalpa (intention), the universe aligns to support your journey. The scarcity of time is an illusion; a powerful Sankalpa attracts all that is needed to achieve your goals. Abundance is a birthright, just as a child seeks nourishment from their parents. The universe and earth provide limitless opportunities, waiting for us to claim them. However, past karma influences our path, and through pure intention and right actions, we can balance and cleanse it. Continuous learning and connection aligning the mind and the heart lead to clarity, intuition, and effortless progress. True leaders are appreciated for their character, not appearance. Success should not be the sole definition of one's identity; instead, it should serve as a tool for personal growth and the ability to contribute to others. When one achieves inner calmness while actively working toward goals, resilience and wisdom follow. This book unveils the hidden qualities that make success sustainable, guiding you towards a life of purpose and fulfillment.

K. KRISHNANANDA

lifemechanism.in@gmail.com

9945715025 / 9811885465

118, IST FLOOR, SECTOR 11D

FARIDABAD

HARYANA

121006

INDIA